CW00363999

Easy Money

How I made my 97 pence

Bob McGregor

Published by
McGregor's Books

ISBN 0 9539200 0 3

Published by McGregor's Books, 35 The Square, Kelso, Roxburghshire, Scotland TD5 7HL
Printed by Kelso Graphics, The Knowes, Kelso, Roxburghshire, Scotland TD5 7BH

Acknowledgements
Heartfelt thanks to the following friends and family:

To my wife, Molly, who smiled sweetly and said nothing when I embarked upon this project - Nothing surprises her any more!

To my daughter, Jackie, who keeps trying to convince me a social conscience is more important than money. Her arguments become unstuck frequently, however, when the pub asks for hard cash, rather than a political diatribe, in exchange for gin and tonics!

To Charlie Denoon, who read the (very) rough draft of my manuscript. He keeps telling me I don't use enough commas, so I've had some printed for the reader - please sprinkle to taste!

,,

,,

,,,

To entrepreneur, Ian McKain, owner of 'Auld Reekie Tours' in Edinburgh, for his generous donation of free entry (for 2 people) to the Ghost, Underground and Witchcraft Tours. The value of the voucher is £16, so you're already going in the right direction - Just by buying this book, you've made some 'Easy Money.'

To Tom Milne, for drawing the wonderful illustrations. I deliberately asked Tom not to make all the characters look like me. My aim is to empower YOU to make money - not to be intimidated by my ability, personality or looks.

And lastly...

A big THANK YOU to everyone who has ever given me money - especially YOU!

Bob McGregor 2000.

Contents

Chapter 1

Wouldn' t it be lovely?

I've anticipated the first questions most readers will ask.

"Are you qualified to write this book?"

All I can say is that I've gone from rags to slightly better rags.

"How much money have you made in your life of ducking and diving?"

I've always made as much as I needed at the time and a little bit extra besides. As a result of this philosophy, I live a comfortable, relaxed life, safe in the knowledge that, if I want any more money, I know how to get some.

Do some serious thinking about money. **DO YOU REALLY WANT IT?** Now there's a stupid question ... or is it? Do you really want money or the things it can buy? The two things are not necessarily intertwined. On a personal 'one to one' basis I often help people to get on the right path to wealth and happiness. I asked a close friend what he wanted money for - "I'd like to live in a big expensive house and drive a classy car," he answered. I found him a job as a chauffeur/companion to one of the sweetest old ladies I have ever met in my life. Now he lives in a big house, drives a Bentley and as a bonus he has a friend whose companionship enriches his life - *wouldn' t that be a lovely story if it was true!*

All I'm suggesting is that you look really hard at what you want. Consider this list of ideas:-

Like shooting outings?...Be a gamekeeper.

Love salmon fishing?...Be a ghillie.

Just want to sit in the sun?...Be a lifeguard.

Enjoy meeting people?...Be a waitress.
(Don' t choose this option if you are a man - there must be better alternatives.)

"Please stop this nonsense... **I WANT MONEY!**"

Before I tell you how to get it, read this prophecy of the Cree Indian People:-

> Only after the last tree has been cut down
> Only after the last river has been polluted
> Only after the last fish has been caught
> Only then will you find that money cannot be eaten.

They say that you can't take your money with you. Well my answer is simple... If that's the case then I'm not going. They also say, "There's no pockets in shrouds." I've thought about starting a manufacturing company to make shrouds with pockets, but I'm told that money is no good to you on the other side. Only goodness and purity of heart is of any value, and these are qualities that only thee and me possess, and I'm not so sure about thee.

There is one way that might be worth a try... before you go, you could leave all your money with me, and we could arrange a special code word. Then if you come back from the other side, I would give you all your money back, less a modest fee for my trouble.

Have I put you off wanting money? If I have, you are not showing enough determination. You have to *really, really* want it. That seems to be the crux of the problem. Most people say they want money, so why don't they make any real effort to get any? In my opinion it's because they feel inadequate in the earnings field, so, if you really want to be rich, you have to tackle your belief in yourself and realise that you have what it takes. You simply haven't developed your full potential up until now.

So when do you start developing this mystical belief in yourself? In your case, I would suggest **NOW** is the perfect time, but I, personally, started as soon as I was able to walk. Because I was the youngest of four children, my parents had realised that little boys didn't have to be wrapped up in cotton wool to survive, so I was given the proverbial inch and I repaid their trust by taking a mile, and then some. At the age of seven, I went on one of my hunting trips after school. The rats in the local council dump were big game to me, and I relentlessly hunted them with stones, bows and arrows and slingshot. Time passes quickly when you're having fun, and I was truly surprised when a police car picked me up at two o'clock in the morning. In response to a 'Mayday' from my parents, they had mounted a search, and eventually spotted me trying to pick out the cat's eyes from the rubber holders in the middle of a country road. The two bobbies, who took me home in their patrol car, were really nice to me, and it was another three years before I found out about the darker side of the men in blue. The next time I had contact with the law, I was taken to the police station and given a severe reprimand, although I had done absolutely nothing wrong. This time, they had come on me by surprise when I was doing a bit of target practice with an air rifle. Two of my little friends were each holding the end of a piece of straw, with fully an inch between their hands, and I was shooting the straw in the gap between. I was quite insulted when the police suggested that I might have injured one of my friends - after all I knew that I was Wild Bill Hickock and Annie Oakley all rolled into one. (I've seen photographs of Annie since, and I was never that butch). I learned a valuable lesson from this episode. If the police were prepared to pick me up and threaten me with a three hundred year jail sentence, when I was completely innocent, what sort of attitude would they adopt if I did something wrong? The freedom that I was given as a youngster allowed me to develop self-sufficiency and the ability to spot opportunities when they arose.

OK, let's get down to the nitty-gritty. If you want money you have to get it from someone else. Who's got it? Everyone has some. You can get it in small amounts from lots of people, or in large amounts from a few people. The latter is usually a bit more difficult because although they say a fool and his money are easily parted, you'll usually find that someone has parted them long before you arrived on the scene. Why would they give it to you? Because you have something they want.

This is where it really starts. What have you got to offer? Talent? Time? Energy? You've got all of these things and a lot more besides. All you have to do is dredge them up and start using them to your advantage.

Let's start with a very simple example and see where it can lead.

I'LL WASH AND VALET CARS ON SUNDAY FOR £20.

You're sitting by the window watching your wife washing your car outside your house. (Positioned to shout the odd word of encouragement and also to tell her if she's missed a bit.) I can almost guarantee some smartie pants will say, "Do mine while you're at it." If you haven't heard that remark, then I find it hard to believe that you have ever washed your car at the roadside. Now is the time for you to rush out and offer your input. You have a choice of replies. You could say "*^^"!+!" or, "Of course she will, just bring it in nearer the hose" or, "It will cost you a fiver"... It was a trick question. The correct response is, "Bring it along every Sunday and she'll wash, wax and vacuum it for £20." The price is not the important thing here. You have turned a casual remark into a money-making opportunity. In other words you are getting into the right frame of mind to make some money, so let's develop this a little further. She already has the hose and the vacuum cleaner out anyway so why stop at two cars? Line up twenty cars at your door. Oops! The neighbours! Wait a minute, I saw twenty cars lined up on my way into town. They were in the car park of a local block of offices. Why don't I offer our services to the staff in there on a weekly basis? How can I get the chance to speak to them all? You don't, you simply put a flier on their windscreen.

"But I don't have a computer to make the fliers."

Don't worry, you can use mine for a tenner, or better still I'll type them for you for twenty." Now don't you dare accept this offer! Your reply should be, "I'll (she'll) wash, wax and vacuum your car as payment." That way you're buying at cost/selling at retail.

It won't be long before you reach the first sticking point. How many cars can she reasonably valet in a week? The answer... As many as you wish. Get organised. You can employ people on a casual basis to take some of the workload, but pay them only on a basis of satisfactory results. Don't let the customer pay your employees or very soon they will become their customers. Try, if possible, to get paid by direct debit or some similar arrangement as this will give continuity to your business.

At some time, you'll meet someone who doesn't want his/her car valeted. "I'm thinking of getting rid of it soon anyway." - What an opportunity!

"What do you fancy next?"

"I'm hoping to find a decent BMW about five years old."

"I think I may be able to help you there. I have a friend who is just about to put his on the market. I'll have a word with him and get back to you."

I'll let the reader fill in the rest of this story.

Don't all rush out and become car washers. I don't want to flood the market (or the car parks). I've simply used this as an example of a thought process that will stand you in good stead. Look at everything around you as an opportunity, and think how you could expand your original idea.

This is what this book is all about:

- Open your mind.
- Spot the opportunity.
- Get started.
- Expand.

Even as I'm typing the first chapter I'm thinking of ways to promote sales of this book. I've written three of four lines, which are absolutely brilliant, so, if anyone is looking over my shoulder, I type these lines and take advanced orders for a copy of the final book. Don't bother looking for the brilliant lines...they had to be deleted to keep the standard consistent throughout the book. I'll fill you in later on the results of this ploy.

Now you've reached the end of chapter one, the question is...should you read on? Personally I wouldn't bother, it's never going to be great literature, but go on anyway....you might just catch an idea that's right for you. Good ideas are infectious you know. If you listen and talk to people who are inspired, it rubs off on you.

(Women readers should substitute wife/husband, he/she in the car wash story. Feel free to pencil in any other alterations you wish throughout the book. You don't have to agree with everything I say, just because I 'm always right.)

Chapter 2
Never miss a trick

'Rich and famous'. I know you want to be rich, because you have bought this book. You shouldn't have done that, because you could have borrowed it from the library, or found it in some millionaire's trash can when he had finished with it. I'll come to that at a later stage in the chapter on wasting money. I've no doubt that some of the readers will be attracted to the idea of being recognised in the street, but I can assure you that it has its drawbacks. For one thing waiters expect bigger tips. Personally, I have decided that the rich part will satisfy me. I've used the photograph of an ugly person in the Author's Biography so that, when this book goes into its fifth reprint, by popular demand, I'll still have my privacy. You must make your own decision on whether you can take all the adulation that following my formula will bring.

Being instantly recognised also has its advantages of course. People like to be seen with anyone who is famous, and will often pay for the privilege. I have yet to see a new attraction like a superstore advertising the fact that the ribbon-cutting ceremony is going to be performed by Mrs. Smith from number 16 High Street because she has a brand new pair of scissors. Even as a famous loser, Eddie the Eagle was able to command large appearance fees to appear on various shows, but he must be the exception to the rule and you will almost certainly have more chance as a famous winner.

In my car-washing story, I've talked about incidents that spark off ideas. Let me take you back to my childhood where this train of thought first started.

I was a very keen angler as a lad and I regularly visited dung heaps to collect worms as bait. Now, by anyone's standards that is not a pleasant pastime, but needs must. A high point for me was when I found two worms stuck together, presumably enjoying a romantic evening for two. That may have doubled my profit margin, but I shouldn't imagine it did much for the worm's courtship.

Fortunately I have no sense of smell, so I was able to turn my handicap into an advantage. Within no time, I had a regular sideline selling worms to the local fishing shop, where they were sold on to people who can enjoy the bouquet of a fine wine or the aroma of a lady's perfume, but don't enjoy "howking in dung heaps." I was rightly proud of my enterprise, but I completely missed the point that I could have started Britain's first wormery, and sold worms to all the fishing shops in the country, and even exported them for agricultural use in areas where the soil would benefit from their tunnelling. **I wish I had written this book earlier so that I could have read it myself!**

Another enterprise I got involved in was catching hedgehogs .... Didn't I have some strange pastimes? I read in a local paper that scientists from the Roslin Institute (yes, the same people who cloned Dolly the sheep) were studying the fleas on hedgehogs to see if they were infecting sheep. Although I was only about twelve years old, I went along to the institute and offered to catch hedgehogs for them. They probably had a good laugh and never expected to see me again, but they offered me six shillings for each one I brought them. That was a lot of money to a twelve year old, and possibly the easiest money I had ever made. I knew that, if you walk along the edge of certain fields at dusk, the hedgehogs are out feeding on the short grass, so I just rolled them into a sack with a stick and delivered them to the Institute. I think they were too embarrassed to say they only wanted a few, and they kept paying me for some time. I was probably earning as much as the scientists, before they had the heart to tell me to stop. The hedgehogs didn't suffer, as the researchers took the fleas and released the hedgehogs again. I probably delivered the same ones a few times, as one of my favourite hunting grounds was quite near their premises.

You have probably guessed I was a country boy and my many money-making schemes included selling fur and feathers in the days when it was not politically incorrect to do so. Again, I stress the point that there are opportunities everywhere, even in the most unusual and unlikely places, so keep yourself aware of what people want, and what they might be prepared to pay for.

The 'politically correct' reference, in the last little story, brings me to a very important point. What are you prepared to do and how far are you prepared to go for money? Think out your parameters and stick to them, rather than spend the rest of your life looking over your shoulder. I'm prepared to sell my body, but so far the only offer I've had is from the cat food factory who say they will buy it by the pound. My wife, Molly, had a very interesting offer when we were in a casino in Spain. I was sitting at the tables, while she was having a drink at the bar, and she rushed over excitedly to tell me that she had just been propositioned.

"A Spaniard thought I was a high class hooker and he was signalling the amount he was prepared to pay me. I think it was two hundred!"

She seemed quite proud about it till I reminded her we were in Spain and two hundred pesetas were worth about a pound sterling. What an insult ... she's worth twice that much! She quickly decided she had misinterpreted the signal and it must have been twenty thousand.

I'm not prepared to do anything very dishonest because anyone who knows me will tell you I'm very pretty, and I don't want to end up as Big Bo's bitch in jail.

It's always better to chose a business that doesn't involve too much paperwork and bookkeeping, as the smell of cooking when you're doing the books can set off the fire alarm. I don't like to employ too many people as I find it difficult to delegate responsibility - that's because I can never find anyone who can do the job nearly as well as I can. Everyone says, "I'd like to be paid what I'm worth." I'd find it very difficult to live on a pittance like that. I'd much rather be paid what *I think* I'm worth, but I'm afraid I'd be pricing myself out of the market.

Dealing with customers is my forte. I find it easy to talk and smile a lot. My wife says it's because I'm married to her, and I must admit she doesn't just make me smile; she has me falling about with laughter at some of the daft things she comes away with. I was selling a small flat recently and the first viewers were a very young couple who wanted it as their first home. My wife, Molly really took to them, and as soon as their offer came in she said,

"I think you should accept it right away, I don't want some rich buggers coming along and outbidding them!"

She is probably the most generous person I know, but she is a real handicap when I'm trying to get rich. I was hoping for a big line of rich buggers all trying to outbid each other. We settled for the first bid, and peace reigned in the McGregor household for another little while. I don't know what she's got against wealthy people, but she has obviously decided that we're not going to join them.

Another little money-spinner fell into my lap when I was doing some door to door canvassing. I noticed that some people were reluctant to answer the door, even although I knew they were in. I thought perhaps they were nervous, as it was quite a rough area, so I had some leaflets printed saying that I could fit a peephole and a safety chain at a very reasonable cost. If I didn't get an answer, I put a leaflet through the door; and if I did get an answer, I mentioned in conversation that they had been a bit quick to answer without knowing who was there. So, either way I had a good chance of getting a sale for my security services.

I'm known as a very lucky person, and many of my money making schemes have just fallen into my lap, but that just seems to happen when you are awake to the possibilities that are all around you.

You may have noticed that most of the ideas I've mentioned are for beginners who do not have a lot of capital available, but, if you are one of the 'rich buggers' my wife talks about, there are shares available in this book. Be warned! The price is going up every time I type another chapter. Before I do, I'm going out to paint the fence. I like watching paint dry, as it allows me to think at my own pace.

Now, let's get down to some of the things that you can do to make a few bob. What have you got to offer that's worth a lot to someone else? It could be years of experience and expertise. You're working for a boss who presumably is making some money by employing you, so you may be able to market that knowledge on a part time basis. That idea doesn't appeal to many people, as they are usually tired of the same thing and want to do something different in their spare time. If, on the other hand, you are thinking of taking the big leap and going full time, it will take some planning. You may need to borrow money from a bank to start a new venture. You could go in with a stocking over your head, or if you are forming a partnership, you could use a pair of tights and go in together. But the best way by far, is to convince the bank manager that you know the business, and you have thought through your plan. Don't try to start at the top, there's only one way to go from there. Good businesses are built, not created. The most impressive businesses usually include some original thinking, or a new slant on an existing idea, so get your thinking cap on. (I'm trying to sell thinking caps here ... that is, after all, what this book is all about).

Another business, that I owned a number of years ago, started, apparently by accident. My brother in law had a small shop and had decided to buy a new shop sign.

"Don't bother," I said, "I'll make one for you."

I was building a fibre glass canoe at the time, and I made his sign out of the same material. It wasn't exactly professional, but it didn't look bad to a blind man running past the shop. His next-door neighbour asked me to make one for him as well, which I did. A few weeks later I had a phone call from a complete stranger saying,

"Are you the sign maker?"

Well to be quite honest, I am the 'anything' when I smell money, so I took his order and decided I'd better learn to make signs. Next time you go out in the street, have a look at how many signs there are around. I was a schoolteacher at the time, but I made signs on a part time basis for a while, before I took the plunge and went full time. The business was a success from the word go, and I was soon supplying signs and lettering all over the country. Because I was not an experienced sign maker I introduced some original thinking into the processes; so there's pros and cons to starting in a new field. (Watch out for the hedgehogs ... they're worth money if you know anyone who wants some fleas). I was able to supply lettering all over the country because the letters were stamped out of sheets of self-adhesive vinyl using blades which looked a bit like pastry cutters. At first I ran these blades through an old fashioned mangle along with the vinyl to press out the letters, but I later converted a motorized engineering stamping machine to do the job, and I was able to stamp out letters at a phenomenal speed. It was at this time that I learned some crude time and motion lessons. If a plastic letter valued at about ten pence fell on the floor, it wasn't worth the time it would take to bend down and pick it up, because the interruption would halt production of another ten letters. **TIME IS MONEY.** If you follow this argument to its logical conclusion, you should follow rich people around in the hope that they will drop a five-pound note, and, if they have read my book, they will realise that they should ignore it and stride on to their next venture. This business was very successful and, although it didn't make me a millionaire, if I had kept the same blade in the machine for long enough I could have been an 'A' millionaire. Shortly after getting into the high-speed letter production I had a phone call from someone who had seen an advert I ran in a national paper. He asked in a very dispirited voice if I could supply twenty thousand black four-inch numbers similar to the type used on car number plates. He had already tried several firms who supply these, and had not found anyone who carried that much stock.

"No problem," I said, "When do you need them?"

"That is the problem," he replied, "I should have ordered them months ago. My firm has to number every joint in a pipe line we have laid, and if we don't finish the work in the next few days there are severe penalty fines for late completion."

When I told him that I could fill his order next morning, he didn't believe me. He knew that no-one had that many black four inch numbers in stock, but I convinced him that it would be worth his while making the two hundred mile trip to my premises. The machine was red hot by the morning, but when he arrived the order was ready for collection, and I was the first person he contacted for all his future orders - sometimes thinking isn't enough and you have to resort to hard work.

Another customer came to my premises and announced,

"Here I am, your furthest away customer ever."

"Where are you from?" I asked.

"California," he said proudly. "I'm on holiday in Scotland."

I turned to one of the men at the bench and said,

"Here's a local lad who thinks he lives far away."

"You've never had a customer from further away than California," he said, so I took him to the door and pointed up to the sky.

"When the moon comes out tonight, look very carefully and you'll see some of our lettering on it."

We had recently supplied some lettering to the space research station in England (probably for their toilet door) but I enjoyed telling someone from California that America wasn't the centre of the universe.

Earlier I mentioned the one handicap that many beginners encounter - lack of capital. There are ways round this, and it's quite often possible to sell before you buy. Ask any businessman if they have stock they would like to unload. The answer will almost certainly be yes. It's not just substandard goods that people want to get rid of, but things that they have not the storage room to keep when they are bringing in new ranges. They may even give you a sample to take away to show potential buyers. The range is limitless, because what might be old stock to a big firm could be exactly what a smaller business is looking for. You could be quite surprised to find that your services are in great demand, once people find out that you are the one with your finger on the pulse. You must become a store of information which both buyer and seller will appreciate. A great deal of this depends on your ability to talk to people and gain their trust, so don't try to con your customers. Let both parties know that you are acting as a middle-man, and you expect to make a fair amount on the deal for yourself. They'll respect you for you honesty, and be prepared to deal with you again in the future. If you develop this ability to speak to people, there are lots of other avenues you can explore. If you like fishing, you could take visitors on trips to your local water. Anglers know the value of local knowledge, and will gladly pay a guide who can show them the hot spots, and advise them on the right fly to use under certain conditions. Let the local fishing shop know what you are doing, so that, when you introduce your clients to them, you can expect to get some commission from the shop owner, as well as your fee from the clients. Even a guided tour of the places of interest in the town would be welcome by most visitors, and a visit to the local library will give you all the information you need to impress them with your knowledge. Get to know the best value restaurants in town, and again you can expect a gratuity from the owner, when your visitors eat there. If you are taking visitors around the town of Kelso, you should always point out that 'McGregor's Bookshop in the Square' will be the highlight of their visit. But don't ask for commission as a kick on the shins often offends. I have given you enough already, by setting you on the road to riches.

Chapter 3
I don' t believe in hard work

Is it possible to have fun while you're working? I know that it must be possible, because I've not been able to retire. Even when I'm having fun I keep finding ways to make it pay, so perhaps I'm not so much working, as playing profitably.

A typical example of this profitable fun idea is home selling parties, where people, particularly women, invite groups of friends to their house to sell some firm's goods. The social aspect of this type of business is very important, because the profit margin is so small for the hostess, that it barely covers the hospitality. There's little doubt that the firm supplying the goods is making a good profit, as the goods are seldom cheap, and the customers feel some obligation to buy, having accepted the hospitality. I hope you are one jump ahead of me in what I'm going to say next. If you're not then go back to page one and start again, but this time pay more attention, and sit up straight and concentrate in my classroom. (If you were two jumps ahead of me please get in touch and let me know where I'm going wrong).

My sister, Evelyn, decided to have a sexy underwear party in her house, selling goods for a very well known organisation. I asked Evelyn to think about how she could increase her profit margin. *Charge more for the goods?* The underwear was already costing about a million pounds per square yard! *Water down the wine?* I'd hate to be at that kind of party when everyone was sober. I offered to come along to the next party to look after the changing room. The offer was declined. Not politely, I might add). It didn't take long to come up with a real solution...Find wholesalers who could supply the type of items needed, buy some samples, then simply take orders (payment is always taken in advance, before the goods are delivered) and pick up what was needed from your supplier. Evelyn is also a pretty handy seamstress so she was able to be the manufacturer, the wholesaler and the retailer for some of the items. I'm surprised she didn't have silkworms working in her spare room.

The same principle can be applied to all sorts of home parties, and it allows you to move away from the traditional lines and try new fields that you have a better understanding of, or a wealth of knowledge about. Not everyone likes sexy underwear, and I personally won't wear anything that lets draughts near my goodies.

Lay this book down now and make a list of the things you could successfully sell at a party, bearing in mind that you should invite the friends who share common interests. (Don't forget to pick the book up again later, otherwise your neighbour, Mr. Jones, might read it and he'll be impossible to keep up with after that.) Here are a few suggestions to start you off -

Children's toys (good one just before Christmas)

Books (invite some local authors... they will be glad of the publicity and be happy to sign copies. If the party is in some exotic location in the South of France remember to invite me.)

Crafts (perhaps you can make some of the goods yourself, and you can certainly find plenty of craftsmen/women who would be glad of an outlet for the product of their hobby.)

Now carry on with your own list and don't be afraid to list ideas which, at first glance may seem a bit far-fetched. With a bit of thought and refinement, even the most outrageous ideas might be the very ones which capture the imagination and interest of your friends. Whatever you are selling, you must make it appear to be very special. If your friends want a tin of beans, they will go to the local supermarket, but you are the only person who is selling magic beans. (If you have any friends called Jack, make sure you have plenty of free space in your garden for the cow, as he may want to barter rather than pay cash). Remember - the magic is in your presentation, so try to sparkle when you are selling, and you will find that your enthusiasm is infectious. There are certain places, where I enjoy shopping, just because the staff are enthusiastic about what they are selling. I know that must be difficult to do when you are selling mundane items, but some shopkeepers still manage it and that really inspires me. My daughter, Jackie and I have a bookshop, and we both love working there because it's so easy to be enthusiastic about books. I believe that people are not what they eat, but they are what they read. Customers are seldom in a hurry when they come in to a bookshop; they like time to browse before they make a purchase, and quite often they come in to have a chat and tell us about what they have been reading. This feedback helps us to stock the right kind of books and recommend them to other people with similar tastes. *I never recommend rubbish unless I've written it myself.* It's easy to strike up a conversation with complete strangers by watching which book they pick up and talking to them about the subject matter. (Better avoided if they happen to be reading the 'Kama Sutra'.) I've often chatted merrily to a customer for a while before I've realised that they are foreign visitors and can't understand a word I'm saying. If a customer is looking at a fishing book I tell them my favourite fishing joke... My brother, Charlie, was fishing in the Junction pool and he caught a six-pound salmon. He was just about to hit it on the head when the salmon looked up at him and said,

"Don't hit me, my name's Rusty and I'm not very big. If you put me back you might catch me again when I grow a bit."

"Well there's a thing," said Charlie, "a talking salmon. My friends are never going to believe this. Well, alright, I'll put you back Rusty, and I hope I'll see you again some day."

Two years later, Charlie was fishing in Junction pool again and he landed an eleven-pound salmon. He was just about to hit it on the head, when the salmon looked up and said,

"Don't hit me Charlie. It's me, Rusty."

"Oh, hello Rusty, it's nice to see you again, but I'm sorry I'll have to hit you this time. You're pretty big now and you'll make a good meal."

"No, no! You mustn't hit me, I'm not just a salmon now, I'm an author and a poet. I've been out in the Atlantic and I've found the wreck of the Titanic, so I'm writing some poems about it. I'm going to call them Titanic Verses by Salmon Rusty."

This is a true story, and all the stories in this book are true, except the ones that aren't. (The Rusty story isn't one hundred per cent true - Rusty was only nine and a quarter pounds, but I'm a fisherman so I rounded up.)

Kelso is a popular town for foreign visitors so I can now tell this story in five languages, but it doesn't improve any in the translation.

Apart from telling my 'Salmon Rusty' joke we try to make the customers feel really welcome in lots of little ways. If they have a dog we tell them to bring it in, but tie their children up to the railing outside. If they do insist on bringing the children in, we insist on a head count on the way in and again on the way out, as they are not allowed to leave any behind. We have a bowl of water and some chews for the dogs. If dogs could read and they had pocket money they would be my favourite customers.

Another bookshop story, which I like, is about a customer who went into one of our competitor's shops and asked for a copy of 'Mein Kampf'.

"Do you happen to know the author?" asked the assistant.

"It was written by Hitler," said the customer.

"Do you know his first name?" said the assistant.

"Really! You must have heard of Adolph Hitler."

"You can't expect us to know all the authors of by heart."

This would never happen in our shop, because we carry the titles, authors and ISBN's of the one hundred and fifty thousand books on the current list in our heads. We still go through the motions of looking up the computer list so that we don't look too smart. I'm pretty sure this ploy works very well, as I have the definite impression that all the customers feel they are superior to me in every way.

Starting a bookshop has been one of my better moves, as it has to be the ultimate place to do a bit of people watching, and that's one of my greatest pleasures in life, since I gave up chasing girls (circa 1900). I could still chase them, but they seem to be so sprightly nowadays that there would be little chance of catching one, and, if I did, I've forgotten what is supposed to happen next. When I see a beautiful girl, nowadays, I want to have her gold-plated and bolt her onto the bonnet of my car as a mascot, whereas at one time I would have wanted to mount her on the bonnet of my car.

If you deal with the public long enough you soon realise that appearances can be deceptive, as was the case recently, when a family consisting of grandma, daughter and little grandson came in together. While the little lad was playing at the toy-box, grandma whispered to me,

"Have you got any naughty videos for sale?"

I was shocked out of my boots... she seemed such a respectable lady, but for all I knew she might have had a starring role in 'Debbie does Dallas' in her younger days. Fortunately for me, her daughter saw my confusion and embarrassment and silently mouthed the word NODDY to me. But for her timely intervention, that innocent little lad might have seen a bed time story that would have kept him awake all night.

If you are doing a job which inspires you, and gives you pleasure, you are much more likely to put in the extra bit of effort, and more importantly, the extra bit of thought that will make it succeed.

Chapter 4
Being skint doesn't matter

Bartering is one of the oldest ways of selling (not to be confused with the oldest trade ... selling true-ish love), and should never be neglected. Remember, when you barter, you are making a sale and a purchase at the same time and you can win on both counts. If you are good at it you'll find that you can increase your profit margin as well as making your sale. Sometimes you will be able to get something you really want for yourself, thus bypassing the nuisance of having to spend money, or you may get an item that you can sell at an even better price. This, unfortunately, leaves you with even more money to spend... nothing's perfect. You will often see ads. in the papers that read,

"Immaculate electric guitar for sale £150 or exchange w.h.y."

The 'w.h.y.' is an abbreviation of *what have you*, and is commonly used by people who like to barter rather than sell for money, although any difference in value can be settled in cash. I answered just such an advert once in a national buying and selling paper. A man in Wales was offering an Aston Martin 'for sale or exchange w.h.y.' I offered him eight thousand sets of darts in exchange for the car, and enclosed a sample pack to let him see the quality. Although he was interested, after he had contacted a few potential wholesalers and market traders, he didn't feel he could shift enough of the darts and the deal fell through. So all my schemes aren't success stories. This might leave you wondering how I came to have eight thousand sets of darts in the first place. I had popped into a small local auction during my lunch hour, on the very remote chance that something interesting might come up for sale. This particular auction usually attracted a handful of elderly ladies whose joint disposable income was about fifty quid, and even that was usually about twice the value of all the items on offer. The list of items being auctioned included eleven boxes of darts and other items. Now, like yourself, I would assume that each box contained three darts, as it's considered to be a bit un-sporting to throw four to try to get one over on your opponent. On this particular occasion, someone who didn't know his arse from his arrow had omitted to say in the advert that each box contained one thousand sets of darts. Apparently, a sports manufacturer had gone bankrupt, and all the stock had been sent to possibly the worst auction house in the country. The auctioneer, give him his due, did the best he could in the circumstances. He split the first box, and sold each of the old dears present, a set of darts at an average price of about fifty pence. Some of them pushed the boat out and bought two or even three sets (in posh games players have their own set), but he was still left with the mammoth task of trying to find a buyer for the rest of the lot. He found me! I bought up the lot at two pence a set, and I was delighted to find it included thousands of spare flights. I stayed on to buy six hundred badminton racquets and six hundred backgammon games in imitation leather briefcases, at comparable prices. I needed three trips in a Transit van to take the lot home - (The second half of the consignment came up for auction the following week, by which time word had gone around the dealers, and the prices increased tenfold). Next morning I sold one thousand sets of darts to a local wholesaler and recovered all the cash I had laid out. For months after that, I was able to make a good living, selling through local ads. to individuals and by direct contact to pubs and clubs. When the deal for the Aston Martin fell through, I took the remainder of the stock to the market trader's wholesalers in Manchester and sold the lot in one day.

A group of people, in my local area, started up a scheme to try to live their whole life by the barter system. They chose the name 'Tweedlets' for their currency as we live beside the river Tweed, and for convenience a 'tweedlet' was given a theoretical value of one pound sterling within our own group. The idea was that any member could obtain goods or services from someone within the group and pay them with 'tweedlets' instead of cash. Let me give you an example which will clarify the system:-John is an old age pensioner who is no longer able to drive, but has a garage attached to his house. He lets the garage to Elaine, a tall beautiful redhead with a captivating smile and the most perfect legs.... sorry, I got carried away... he lets the garage to Elaine for five 'tweedlets' a week. John's account is now in credit, and he can spend his five 'tweedlets' with any other member of the group. For instance he can ask Ian who is a qualified carpenter to make him a new wooden leg at a cost of seventy-five 'tweedlets'. Does that mean that he will have to hop around for fifteen weeks before he can afford to take delivery of his new leg? Of course not! He can allow his account to go into the red until he earns some more 'tweedlets'. Meanwhile Ian asks Elaine for certain services and she tells him to piss off, so he approaches Tom the chicken farmer who supplies him with a dozen eggs a week at a cost of two 'tweedlets'. Tom gets two pheasants and half a dozen rabbits from the Jim the gamekeeper, but the Chancellor of the Exchequer doesn't get a pound of flesh because he didn't join the 'Tweedlets' scheme. Now it's all starting to sound a slightly complicated, a bit like the Old Testament when all the begetting was going on. At that time, someone must have been watching and writing it all down in preparation for writing his book, 'Who's Begetting Who in the Middle East'. In the 'Tweedlets' scheme, we had a scribe with a computer, who made up a monthly list of everyone's spending and earnings, and the credit or debit balance of their account. The beauty of it was, that it didn't matter a damn if it was accurate at all, because it wasn't real money anyway. Our scribe/accountant was paid in 'tweedlets' and the most important thing in his monthly newsletter wasn't the balance, but the list of goods and services that the members had to offer. It's amazing what you'll try if it doesn't cost real money.... I found out from a colour therapist that I wouldn't suit blue eye shadow but I would cause quite a stir if I went out in gold lamé trousers, and I discovered from a past life practitioner that I was once Richard the Lionheart. (I wouldn't have given him any 'tweedlets' if he had told me that I was someone very ordinary.) I wonder if someone in the year two thousand and fifty will be told,

"You were Bob McGregor in a previous life. That will cost you five hundred 'tweedlets'."

I liked the 'Tweedlets' bartering system in principal, but its success depended very much on the skills of the members. Too many stone circle dancers and not enough plumbers and house painters could leave you feeling that, even for free, you didn't want the services on offer. Here's a list of possible skills, goods and services that could be on offer:

Elaine...Children's parties arranged and supervised; Personally designed cakes baked for special occasions; Baby-sitting.

Tom...Shooting instruction; Rough shooting days for rabbits; Cross country 4 wheel driving.

Ian...Furniture hand-made to your specification; Extending ladders and power tools for hire; Lessons in carpentry from beginners to expert standard.

William...Emergency plumbing repairs; Fitting garden sprinkler systems; Landscaping.

Sarah...Car trips to the shopping complex Mon, Wed and Fridays; Sewing alterations; Wedding dresses made to order.

Jim...General labouring; Simple household repairs; For sale...C.D. player in good working order... 30 'tweedlets'.

Ryan and Betty...Holiday cottage to let during low season - 40 'Tweedlets' per week.

Bob...Best selling books written, while you wait; Blackjack instruction; Guitar lessons for pre-beginners standard; Base metals turned into gold; For sale...anything I've got, if the price is right; Modelling for 'before and after' adverts; Instruction on how to make Easy 'Tweedlets'; Trailer for sale or rent; Rooms to let 50 cents.

If you keep adding to that list you could find everything you want in life and its all free. All you have to do is offer something in return which needn't cost you any money at all. If something is missing from the list that you want, then find a new member who can offer it and encourage them to join the group. This system doesn't just appear out of thin air, it needs someone to initiate it. Why not you? You can start with a few friends and its amazing how quickly it will catch on. There's a social side to it as well. You can hold monthly meetings in the back room of your local pub to discuss new ideas, and introduce new members, or have table-top sales where the goods are on sale to the public, for cash, or to the members, for 'Tweedlets'. This is also the ideal time to increase the membership as the visitors will immediately see the advantages of bartering goods and services. If you are an immature adult like myself, then why not relive your past by recreating Blue Peter's Bring and Buy Sales' and taking part in your own multi-coloured 'Swap Shop'?

Chapter 5
If you' ve got it, flaunt it

I hope you have been able to find some interesting and useful pointers in the preceding chapters, but more than that, I hope you have been inspired to think of some new ideas or some new slants on old ideas. It may all have been done before, but never with the flair and originality, which you are going to give it. Before you try to sell, think of any reasons that your customer might have for not buying now, then think of ways to overcome that problem. A typical example, in my life, was when I hired video films from a van, or rather from a converted ambulance, which I had racked so that the film boxes could be displayed around the walls like a shop. The customers could walk into the ambulance, choose their films in comfort, and rent any three films for a week for £5. As a further incentive the customer did not pay the hire price when they rented the films, but when they returned them one week later. At first sight, this system would seem to have an obvious weakness, in that the customer might be reluctant to part with the money, after they had watched the films. However, unless they paid, they could not hire any more films, and that was usually enough incentive to make them pay. On the odd occasion that someone avoided paying, I had lost a customer who was unlikely to be a regular in any case, and it wasn't long before I had established a regular reliable clientele. The concept of 'watch now and pay later' was novel enough to interest new customers to join, and since they were out at my van paying for last week's films, they felt they might as well hire another three for next week. I don't claim that this concept was earth shattering and Einstein may have said, "So what?", but he couldn't even set the timer on a video recorder, so I don't really give a damn what he would have thought, as long as it worked for me.

You may not even be aware of the ways in which subtle techniques are used to encourage you to buy certain goods in some of the larger stores. Many large firms employ experts to look at the slightest changes that can be made to increase sales, and even more importantly, to increase profitability. A very famous confectionery outlet sprays the smell of chocolate in the shop to stimulate your saliva glands, although all their products are carefully sealed to preserve their freshness. In most supermarkets there are items displayed near the checkouts, which are known as impulse buys, and they weren't placed there by accident. Photos of scantily clad women are used to advertise all sorts of men's goods and, although I am immune to this technique, it must have some measure of success as it is so widely used. Men should ignore the superficial dressing and try to see what is underneath it all.

When you are shopping in less professional surroundings, watch the sales person and try to imagine how you could improve on their methods. Sometimes, even the simplest things, like a laugh and a joke, could help them make a sale, but, if you are a sour-faced git, then you'll have to work out an alternative plan.

A less subtle technique for selling the idea of American superiority was used by the CIA in their psychological warfare against the Viet Cong. They dropped presents of condoms for the enemy soldiers, and these were size XXL that would have been a loose fit on a three-year old Clydesdale horse. These had been specially produced to give the enemy soldiers an inferiority complex. I don't know how successful this ploy was, but I know I would have been really worried, if I thought that the guy who was dropping the bombs from his plane had a really big willie.

I keep using the word 'subtle' in this chapter for very good reason. No-one is going to believe that the second-hand car that you are selling has only had one previous owner - a nun who only used it when she was driving to and from wife swapping parties, (hence the very low mileage), but simple things like replacing worn mats and spraying the interior with a leather smell could influence a potential buyer. Leave a couple of golf tees lying in the car and the buyer will think it's a de-luxe model. (If you don't understand the significance of *this*, ask a more-worldly friend. Its number 197 in the schoolboy's elementary joke book.)

All of these selling ideas lead us naturally on to advertising, and the story here is... **IF YOU'VE GOT IT, FLAUNT IT**. Big companies spend a large proportion of their budget on promoting their brand name, and it works! Have you ever '*hoovered*' your carpet with an Electrolux vacuum cleaner? I bought a full set of well known brand name weight training equipment, and, if I ever build up enough strength to open the packaging, I'm convinced I'll have a body like Arnold Schwarzenegger, because the advert said it was so. A large proportion of your budget may be next to sod all, but a lot of advertising can be obtained even at that modest price. An unlettered van is a waste of advertising space, and even if you are using your car, why not have a magnetic sign, which you can use when you are trading, and stow in the boot when you want to use the car socially? If you can link your product to some human interest story, you might be able to encourage a local newspaper to print an article without paying advertising rates e.g. Bob McGregor, the owner of a Kelso bookshop, fell from the top of the Blackpool Tower whilst on holiday. His last words were, "We carry a very good range of Scottish Border books in our shop." Now that may seem a little bit too extreme, but you get the idea. A few years ago I was promoting an indoor market in my premises and decided to print some advertising leaflets, so instead of bearing the cost myself, I sold space on the leaflet to several other local businesses at a price which would cover the printing and distribution costs. I also towed a trailer with some eye-catching advertising and a large cut-out of Mickey Mouse on it. The cut-out had absolutely nothing to do with the business, but it caught a lot of attention and made passers-by look at the adverts. The business was a complete failure, and closed after a very short time, which shows that even a genius, like I think I am, can get it wrong sometimes. The person who never made a mistake, never made anything, and the important thing is to analyse and learn. When Molly and I have a disagreement I always admit that I'm wrong right at the start, and that saves a lot of time and effort.

The most important thing about advertising is to reach the right people, that is, the people who may be interested in your product or service. A radio station will gladly sell you a time slot to advertise hearing aids, but a visual approach might be a better option for you in this case. If you are repeatedly selling the same product, then give it a name, which is exciting and trips off the tongue, like 'Easy Money'. Doesn't that title make you want to rush out and buy another copy as soon as you finish reading this one?

If you are a shopkeeper, then your window is your first point of sale, and it is worthwhile spending a bit of time and effort making your display attractive to the public. If you are not particularly talented in this direction, then look around at the other windows in town, pick the best one, approach the person responsible for the display, and ask him/her if they will do yours in exchange for something really valuable, like your eternal gratitude.

Catchy slogans may do the trick and I was very impressed with an advert used by an Indian- owned firm of builders which read, 'Are you fed up with cowboy tradesmen? Why not try the Indians?' Another impressive ad. was placed in a building trade journal by a girl called Fifi and it read 'Temporary erections demolished.'

The most effective advertising of all is word of mouth and it is probably the hardest kind to get. You can't buy it, and the way to achieve it is by making sure you leave a trail of satisfied customers behind you, (I'm sure Fifi did.) Whose name springs to mind when you are looking for something? The one you saw in an ad. in the paper or the person who was recommended by a happy customer? Think about that when you are dealing with people and you will reap the rewards in the long run. I keep a box of chocolates in the shop for free-spending customers that I really like. The token is more appreciated than discount (and it's cheaper), and, if I don't have a suitable customer for a while, I eat them myself because I really like me.

I mentioned at the end of Chapter One that I had started to promote sales of this book, so to this end I now have a sign in the shop, which reads:

BOB IS SELLING A BOOK THAT DOESN'T EXIST

Feel free to read a few extracts, make comments and place your order for a copy now.

Here are a few of the responses I have had so far;-

Bill Gates... "I certainly want a copy. I can't wait to read the rest of the book and then I can start to make some real money."

Gordon Brown, Chancellor of the Exchequer... "This book could be the foundation of New Labour's financial policy for many years to come. Utopia is just around the corner. We are determined to make sure that every man and woman in this country has enough disposable income left, after taxation, to be able to afford to buy a copy of this book." (I had to cut short the Chancellor's comments at this stage, as they went on for three hundred and ten pages, but he finished off with a rousing chorus of 'The people's flag is pastel pink').

Peter Mandleson... "I've turned the pages round and round and I can't find any way to put more spin on them." (Because of his failure he was removed from his position as spin-doctor and sent to Northern Ireland.)

Julia Roberts... "I regret having walked into the wrong bookshop. The film could have been called 'Kelso Square' instead of 'Notting Hill', and the love scenes would have been much more convincing. I know it goes against the spirit of the book but I would have been prepared to take a huge cut in my salary." (Julia doesn't have to buy a copy because I'd like to give her one.)

George Thomas B.A.(Hons) B.Sc. (Hons) M.A. Ph.D. ABC,DEF,GHI. "I'm going to buy a copy because I feel that it will improve my education."

A. Scrooge... "I'll even buy a copy when it is remaindered."

Mr. Spock. (U.F.O. investigator) "We want to look further at this new advanced way of thinking, as we feel that it may have strange origins."

R. Thompson (critic)... "Einstein, Da Vinci, McGregor. I can't spot the odd one out."

Mrs. Blackface-Ewe... "I go along with everything that has been said so far."

Tommy Wells (Council Cleansing Department)... "Waste-paper collections are Mondays and Thursdays."

In one, or more, of the above cases, the names of the people concerned may have been changed to protect their privacy, and I may have used poetic licence (less sophisticated readers may call it lying) in recording their comments.

Chapter 6
Make me an offer

Selling your business is an interesting option, particularly if you enjoy starting something new and find after a while that it becomes tedious. I have sold several businesses in my life, and I'm glad to say that the purchasers have taken them forward in the long run. I enjoy the challenge of a new venture, but many people feel more comfortable taking over an established concern without the risk element. If you feel that way, you don't have to wait for a business to come on the market, you can approach anyone who is trading, and ask them if they would be interested in selling to you. There is an established formula for pricing a business which takes into account the turnover and the profitability over a period of years, and it is well worthwhile seeking professional help if you are not experienced.

If you are selling, the best time is when the business is 'on the up'. Your buyer should feel that there is a good foundation to build on. If you are buying, have a good look at the employees, particularly in the retail trade, as they are your vital link with the customers. When I'm serving in the bookshop I sometimes have customers who ask in a very disappointed voice, "Is Jackie not in today?" and I feel I should apologise for being me. She has obviously established a rapport with people who want to talk about academic subjects like art and philosophy, and aren't interested in hearing the latest daft joke from me.

If you are a buyer, make sure you have written, into the contract, that the seller will not set up a similar business within a specified time or distance from your premises, otherwise you could find that they take the best customers with them.

If you are buying the business, but not the premises, have a good look at the lease and even discuss it with the landlord as the rent may be increased, or, even worse, may be terminated shortly after the sale. Get an agreement in writing! I have a very wise solicitor who repeatedly tells me, "Bad ink is better than a good memory."

I have known businessmen who start a business with the express intention of selling it within a very short period. There is nothing immoral about this practice as their particular talent may be their ability to get the business off the ground from scratch, and the sale price may well exceed the profit they have made whilst they were building it up. A business doesn't have to be big to be sellable, but it has to suit the buyer, and it may be that your market stall pitch will be in more demand than a factory with a hundred employees. If you have spotted a gap in the market, and built up a clientele, then your efforts should be reflected in the sale price.

"What kind of business should I buy?"

The answer is definitely one that you know something about. It's not a good idea to buy a gun-shop, if you don't know which end of the gun the bullet comes out from, although you may be able to find out by trial and error. I can offer some excellent (though slightly biased) advice if you want to buy a bookshop in the Scottish Borders, and unlike the gun scenario you won't come to any harm if you read the books backwards - try it with this one - it may even improve it.

How about buying a business, which is failing miserably? On the plus side it will be cheap - maybe even free, if you purchase the stock at cost. It still doesn't seem like a good idea, does it? Let me tell you a story about a girl I met in Spain. Louise had been doing the usual tourist thing - wandering along the front looking at shops selling souvenirs - key-rings shaped like willies, T-shirts with rude messages, donkey ornaments etc. There were forty-seven similar shops in the row, and, despite the throngs of tourists, none of them were making much money because of the competition. (Even the British holiday-makers can only buy a limited amount of crap to take home to their friends.) When she had bought her allotted quota she started chatting to the shopkeepers.

"How's business?" she would ask.

"Terrible! The British don't buy nearly enough of my high quality crap," or words to that effect.

Fortunately she had brought her thinking cap with her, which saved her having to buy a sombrero with 'I'm Pissed' on the hatband. She selected a tiny shop, which had not yet floated its shares on the stock market, and said to the shopkeeper,

"How would you like to sell your business?"

There was a stream of rapidly spoken Spanish which, roughly translated, meant,

"Olé! You must be the stupidest person I have ever met. You will pay me ten times what it's worth. I can then buy a costume and become a famous matador in Madrid."

After a great deal of arm waving and gnashing of teeth, Louise bought the business for the wholesale price of the stock. The shelving and other fittings were thrown in for the price of a large tin of 'Elastoplast' - to be used during his training period in the bullfighting ring.

So far this doesn't seem like a very shrewd business move, does it? Well, the shop was in a good location. It had a little room at the back with a bed, cooker and a kettle. What was really needed was a change of stock, and that's exactly what Louise had in mind. Before she left the U.K. she had bought two of the latest novels. She had read one on the beach and the other in her hotel room on the one day that it had rained. Now she was looking for something to read without success. Ping! A new idea was born. Having bought the 'El Spanish Crapo' shop she went round the holidaymakers in her hotel and scrounged all the paperbacks which they had read. No-one wanted to take them back home, as their suitcases were full of 'unwanted gifts' for their friends. Now Louise sits in a sun-lounger in front of her shop for seven months of the year and makes enough money to spend the remaining five months back home. She never has to buy stock. Most holiday makers are delighted to give her the paperbacks they have read, in exchange for a willie shaped key-ring or some equally valuable piece of authentic Spanish memorabilia.

Chapter 7

The only thing that grows in size after it's dead

I've lost this chapter completely, although I know that I've written it. I have two computers, one at home and one in the shop, and, when I've written a piece on one of them, I e-mail it to the other computer, or I copy it on a floppy disk and transfer it to the other machine. I don't know if it will ever turn up, and I've been advised not to go looking for it inside the computer with a hammer and a screwdriver. So I'll re-write it now and, although this makes it a second-hand chapter, you will still be charged the full price for it when you buy the book. I had a bout of writer's block (a sort of mental constipation) when I was writing this part and I decided that it was because I was thinking too much about money, so I called this chapter 'Easy Fish' instead of 'Easy Money'.

You will have gathered that I'm a country boy and I love my fishing. I have a sign in my room that says, 'A days fishing adds an extra day to your life,' and I intend to live forever. (If this book is published posthumously, this will be one of the very few times that I have been wrong.) I won't tell you everything I know about the sport, otherwise you will catch so many fish that you will be supplying the local fishmonger, and you will have the problem of finding places to store all your cash. Don't keep stuffing it under the mattress or you'll hit your head on the ceiling when you are getting into bed. Instead, I'll be like the chap who came home from a very wild stag night with a cup inscribed '1st. Prize in the Biggest Willie Competition'. His wife was horrified and said,

"You didn't show them that thing of yours, did you?"

"Of course not," he said, "I just showed enough of it to win the prize."

When I've explained the basics to you you'll be able to say,
"With my superior intellect I have been able to outwit a fish." (A shoal of grayling has an I.Q. of about eighty and they have to share it between them.)

If you decide to buy a book about fishing, take it to the riverside and read it out loud so that the fish will understand exactly what they are supposed to do. Your first stop will be at the local tackle shop where you will spend so much money that you could have bought enough fresh filleted fish to fill your freezer several times over. You must buy the latest high power rod so that you can cast your fly right across the river to the fish feeding near the far bank. (Why not drive round by the bridge and drop your fly over that bank without the least bit of effort?) Most of the tackle you buy will be to impress other fishermen, rather than the fish, but I've found an even better way to really impress them. I set out very early in the morning and catch a few good trout, using all my expensive equipment. I lay these trout on the bank in plain view, hide my rod and tackle, and start fishing with a broken branch with a piece of string tied to the end of it. Then I dangle the most ridiculous looking fly in the water near my feet. Other fisherman who are passing never say a word, but I can see the frustration in their faces, and I quietly enjoy the joke until they are out of sight. (The Marquis of Sade could take lessons from me when the devil's in me.)

Now that you have bought your tackle you may feel that you are ready to start fishing, but you have some serious homework to do first. You must learn all the excuses for not catching anything, after thrashing the water all day. Here is a list of some of the more useful ones:

1) The sun was too bright.

2) The wind was blowing from the east (or west, north or south as appropriate.)

3) There are otters in the river eating all the fish (or herons, pike or great white sharks, as appropriate).

4) It was too hot, cold, wet, dry, thundery. (T.V. weather presenters can probably go into much   greater detail on this one.)

5) My flies were not right. (By the time I zipped them up the fish had stopped feeding.)

6) The water level was too low. (Or high or wet).

7) The fish were so big that they bit through the steel hawser I was using as a line.

8) I broke my rod. (Or leg, heart, etc.)

9) I'm not a very good fisherman. (This one is seldom used).

10) The village idiot had got there before me with a broken branch and a piece of string and caught all the fish.

There are lots of other excuses available and your best bet would be to consult my brother Charlie, who is much more of an expert on these matters than I am. (Practice makes perfect.)

Most fishermen will tell you that the bag is not the important thing, it's the enjoyment of nature and the solitude that gives fishing its appeal. I've watched them soaking wet, with icicles on their noses and I realise how much they are enjoying the great outdoors. None of them will admit they are fanatics, not even the chap who married his girlfriend after the doctor told her that she had worms. (There's nothing wrong with a bride having a dowry!)

Now you are ready to make your first approaches to the waterside. Assemble your rod, fix on your line and open your box of flies. Before selecting your fly, try to think like a fish ... which fly would you most like to eat? The fish probably thinks, "That fly looks smaller than me so I'll eat it." On the other hand the fish may see you and think, "He looks bigger than me so he might eat me." The only other combination possible is that the fish thinks, "That fisherman looks smaller than me, I think I'll eat him." If this is the case you should take certain steps... great big rapid ones, until you are a long way from the water.

Persevere with your efforts and you will hook tufts of grass, wire fences, your own ear and, with a huge amount of luck, perhaps a fish. This makes it all worth while and you'll soon realise that it wasn't you hooking a fish, but the fishing bug hooking you for life.

I've got that out of my system now, so I'll get back to writing 'Easy Money'.

Chapter 8
Fancy being a gypsy?

At some time in your life, you will find yourself in the property market, although for most people it only involves buying or selling their own home, and this may only happen half a dozen times in your life. With a change of attitude, this can be the biggest opportunity you will ever have to make lots of money. Instead of thinking of it as your home, think about it as your most valuable trading asset. From the minute you buy your house, you must consider it to be for sale again if someone offers you the right price. Try to buy at the best possible price and avoid the temptation of falling in love with the house and paying more than the market value as a result of your infatuation. Leave that mistake to the next purchaser. Obviously, you will want to make improvements to any house you buy, but you must make these changes with prospective buyers in mind. Try to increase the value and selling potential of the property by at least as much and preferably more than the amount you are spending. This is more likely to be the case if you can do at least some of the work yourself rather than paying the prices that professionals will charge, but be aware of your limitations and only tackle what you are confident of doing safely.

The reason that your own home is your best asset is that any profit that you make when you sell is absolutely tax-free. This is only the case if the house is your main residence.

There are several ways of buying at the right price. Firstly you can make an offer on a house which is not yet on the market, if you know that the present owners want to move. They may be emigrating, or want to move to a different part of the country, and be dreading the complications of marketing their house, and be unsure of how long it will take to find a buyer. For some people the thought of complete strangers tramping through their home is quite upsetting, especially knowing that the majority of viewers are not genuinely interested in purchasing, but simply passing a bit of time. By selling to you, they also save the expense of advertising and the fee that an estate agent would charge, so they might accept a considerably smaller offer to simplify the selling process.

At the other end of the scale, you can make a low offer on a house that has been on the market for some time and has not yet found a buyer. If you are using this method, try to find out why this is the case. It may be something you can put right before you come to sell at a later date, but if there is some inherent problem, like unpleasant neighbours, then you will have the same problem in front of you at some time, and this has to be reflected in the price. (I've just realised why my neighbours keep offering me the use of their holiday cottage. They must be trying to sell their house while I'm away on holiday.) More often a house has not sold quickly because of bad presentation, and a few weeks work with a scrubbing brush, a coat of paint and some imagination will transform it into a Des. Res.

House auctions have to be considered, but I have had some unpleasant experiences in this area. Last year, I received a catalogue from an auctioneer, which listed about forty houses which were going under the hammer at the end of the month. I was interested in three of the properties, so I went to the expense of having them surveyed and valued, and, armed with that information, I attended the sale. The bidding was brisk and the first two houses went well over the price I was prepared to pay but, on the third one, I appeared to have only one competitor. When I stopped bidding, the house was knocked down to the next bid. I went home a bit disappointed, but I felt that I had learned from the experience. Little did I know what I would learn in the next few days. In Scotland a bid is legally binding as soon as it is made, so I was very surprised to receive a phone call from the auctioneer's office offering me the same property for the amount of my last bid. My suspicions were aroused. Did my competitor actually exist or was the auctioneer 'taking bids off the wall?' If there was someone else bidding, was he a stooge making bids to push up the price? I never managed to get satisfactory answers to my queries, and the whole episode confirmed my belief that there are some very sharp cookies in property marketing. Needless to say I refused their offer to purchase. If there are lots of bids you may have the three stooges bidding against you.

If you decide to make money by selling your home regularly, there are a few basic rules, which will be useful:

Don't gather too many possessions. That will make moving easier.

Have a few really good pieces of furniture. Although these aren't being sold with the house, it gives the best impression to prospective purchasers.

Have arrangements in place to store your possessions, if you get the chance of a good sale for your home, before you have a new place in mind.

Be prepared to live in rented accommodation, or even a caravan, until you can buy your next property at the right price.

Have a plausible explanation why you are selling. "I don't like living next door to Bob McGregor," may be true, but try to think of one, which won't put your buyer off.

The important thing to remember, if you want to make money this way, it's a bit of a gypsy lifestyle, but the potential profits are high and you don't have to give your forwarding address to people you don't like.

If you have capital to spare, buying houses, shops or even garages to rent out or re-sell can be a good investment. The same basic rules apply. Buy at the best possible price and try to select areas, which are on the up. Although highly profitable, the basic problem with renting out your property is finding good tenants. Good tenants are the ones who pay their rent in full, and on time, every month, keep the place in good order and stick rigidly to the lease agreement. Don't underestimate the value of making sure the lease agreement covers every possible eventuality. If you are successful in getting a good tenant, you will be earning regular income while hopefully your property is increasing in value.

Chapter 9

The pen is mightier than the penknife, or something

Have you ever considered writing for profit? Jeffrey Archer has written books to get him out of financial difficulties. I owe the local newsagent £1.45 for deliveries and I am hoping to clear this debt from the profit on this book. I had other alternatives in mind, like becoming a world champion snooker player, or an internationally famous footballer, but both of these options required a little physical effort and possibly even some talent, so I decided that writing rubbish was a better alternative for me.

It has been suggested that there are more people writing books than there are people buying them, and those who are not actually putting pen to paper are toying with the idea for some future date. Folklore has it that everyone has a book inside of him/her, waiting to get out. When many of these books do get out, they should be forcibly re-inserted into the authors at the earliest opportunity, but usually a simple rejection by the publishers will end the book's life, before it sees the light of day. Don't be put off by the fact that you may not be successful on your first attempt. If you get rejection letters you will be joining very illustrious company. I am one of the very few authors who have never had a rejection letter, but that record may only last until I submit a manuscript. (No! No! I hear you cry)

I gave my sister, Evelyn, this book to review at this stage. She settled down to read it with a nice box of chocolates beside her and her report was very positive. She particularly enjoyed the soft centres. She says that she will enjoy the rest of the book if I give her a bottle of Chianti to drink while she is reading it. I'm grateful for that kind of feedback. It makes it all worthwhile knowing that my future as a writer is assured.

Have a look at the shelves in a bookshop - preferably mine. People write about some very strange subjects, and even stranger, other people actually buy the books and read them. They're not all best sellers, and the authors may barely cover their costs, but be happy to have the satisfaction of getting into print with their pet subject or theory. The crucial point is to ask yourself what you are aiming for. Is it fame and lots of cash, or just enough to cover the cost of your paper, envelopes and stamps? If you go for the jackpot, you may finish up with nothing, whereas an article about gardening in the local papers, a story about local history, or a short story written in local dialect could bring in a modest return and has a much greater chance of success.

There is a kind of profit that is worth considering. You may achieve a tiny measure of fame. People who know you, may think that as a writer you can be classed alongside the Archers, the Cornwells, and the Collins'. On the other hand, they may think of you as a lazy sod, who can't be bothered doing any real work. Real work, to some, involves more than just scribbling. Test this out by telling a new acquaintance, as modestly as you can, that you are a writer. Watch his eyes glaze over. They will light up again when he tells you that Miss Graham marked one of his essays at school nine out of ten. That was thirty years ago, when he was eleven, but he hasn't forgotten, and knows full well that he could pick up a pen and write a book any time he chose, but he's far too busy with real work to be bothered at the moment. It's more the kind of thing he'll do in retirement.

However, you can turn your little bit of local fame into cash if you are willing to speak publicly about your writing, or more particularly about your subject areas. Get on the list of speakers available for W.I., Townswomen Guild, Rotary, Retirement Clubs, etc. They will pay you and often provide a nice meal into the bargain when you are billed as the main attraction of the evening. Sounds easy, doesn't it? Beware! All voluntary organisations have secretaries who pride themselves on being able to persuade speakers to perform for little more than travel expenses. Some can even conjure up speakers from local friends and relatives and save even these little expenses. I know one speaker who generously waived his fee. He was puzzled when the secretary insisted on knowing what he would have charged.

"About fifty pounds, but why ask if I'm doing it for nothing?"

The secretary smiled, and said, "I have a system. When I can get a speaker for nothing I put what he would have charged into a fund so that we can afford a really good speaker occasionally."

Make sure you are one of the really good speakers. Try to build your reputation as someone knowledgeable and entertaining. No matter how serious your subject, a little humour will go a long way to giving your audience an evening to remember. Try to get to know, in advance, a little bit about some of the members of the group and direct some of the humour at individuals who can enjoy a laugh at their own expense. I had occasion to speak to a group of Rotarians recently, and although I was introduced as the speaker, nobody had been told my subject. These lads all looked young and fit (I don't know what happens to old Rotarians), so, over dinner, I told them that, in my army days, I had taught unarmed combat. There was an atmosphere of expectation and a little trepidation when they arrived in the lecture room after the meal. I had slipped through a little ahead of them and, when they arrived, I was dressed in a Stetson and cowboy boots. I told them that I had looked them over, and decided that I felt line dancing would be better suited to their abilities. There were roars of laughter when I chose one of the macho characters, who had enthused about the idea of unarmed combat, to come to the front, and lead the line dancing with me. They all joined in, with hoots of laughter throughout the session, and we settled down to talk about my more conventional subjects later in the evening. I can turn my hand (and my feet) to a few different things.

ROUGHEST, TOUGHEST
BALLERINAS IN THE WEST

You can titillate with some slightly risqué material, but choose your material wisely, according to your audience. Speaking to a group of young medical students, on the serious subject of circumcision in certain cultures, you might say,

"I'll give you the broad outline of the subject before dinner, but I'll leave you a few little snippets to chew over with your coffee."

If you say you are going to use slides and other visual aids, make sure your flies are done up before you stand up, or you could end up starring in Candid Camera. On the other hand the word 'bum' might be enough to startle and amuse a group of girl guides.

Back to writing for profit. Can you write at all? Yes? Good. Well what are you going to write about? Anything and everything? Wrong answer, if you hope to be doing articles for newspapers and magazines. These publications have their own staff writers who can fill the spaces quite easily. Far better to specialize on a subject you really know in depth. Editors will start to approach you when you have built your reputation, and they need an article which they know you can write with authority.

You fancy having a go at the big money? All right, let's list a few of the possibilities:

Crime Stories? - There's a huge readership and regular sales. Go for it, especially if you have a new angle on crime or specialist knowledge, perhaps as an ex-policeman or even as an ex-villain. If you are a current villain, it may not be a good idea to give away the plot of your present enterprise, especially if you are going to give times and places. Some of the police force will be able to read. Any snags in this kind of writing? Yes. There are thousands of aspiring writers trying to emulate Agatha Christie, P.D. James et al. The competition is fierce but the rewards are there for the lucky few.

Science Fiction? - Another good one. There are millions of enthusiasts, but the snag is that they have become very sophisticated and look for some believable science in their Sci-Fi. Next time you are abducted by aliens, ask them for some hard facts, and, if possible, a few photographs, preferably clear ones that leave nothing to doubt. You could have a best seller on your hands.

Horror Stories? Only if you are stable and down to earth. If you are inclined to start believing what you write, you could end up in very comfortable accommodation being looked after by people in white coats.

Mild Pornography? - Check the top shelves of the newsagent's. There is no point in saying you are researching a book. They have heard it all before; so best to say 'nowt' and let them reach their own conclusions. Considerate shopkeepers will supply a set of steps with a label saying 'Steps for short perverts.' Everyone imagines that his/her own sexual experience is special, if not entirely unique. Is yours such that the world will want to read about it? Ask your spouse. Hollow laughter is a bad sign. I am so helpful that I have been told that I should be knighted in the Honours List. In fact this has been said on five occasions so I could have been known as Sir Robert (five times a knight) McGregor - So much for wild fantasy. You'll make it all up, you say. Try it. Then read your own work, in private, and see if you can cope with the embarrassment of even writing any more, far less having it read by your friends.

Pseudo-Psychology? - Advice for the love-lorn, the troubled, the confused and the downright nutty finds space in publications of all kinds. Comfortably plump middle aged women, earnest austere ladies in straight black dresses, and even men in floral shirts with delicate manners are all busy star gazing, chart reading and dishing out advice to millions. Jump in, the water's lovely and there's always room for one more.

Love and Romance? - Now you're talking. All the world loves a lover, and we desperately need more heroes who are not exactly handsome, but have strength in their chiselled features. Add in a sprinkling of wealth and property, and a few heaving bosoms and you could be on your way to joining millions of others who are writing the same story almost word for word. Yes, again the competition is fierce. How many kitchen table writers do you know who are writing romantic fiction? I know five. I asked Jackie and she knew my five and two others. Molly knows another two and her two even know each other.

I could go on ad infinitum, I suppose, but you see the point. It can be tough but if you persist there can be tremendous satisfaction and, for the lucky few, financial rewards. Search your own experience and imagination. Use the 'Writer's and Artist's Yearbook' to research the kind of agents and publishers who may be interested in your kind of stuff. Sit down and write. Wait for the cheques or the rejection slips. That is it. There's no secret, no mystery. Succeed or fail. You'll never know until you try.

Chapter 10
Almost new (ten years ago)

I love car boot sales. It's all there. Priceless antiques for two quid and you can even haggle that down to three for a fiver, and they will throw in a pair of rusty hinges that almost fit your garage door. I once bought a painting by Stradivarius and a violin made by Van Gogh. It wasn't until I had them valued by an expert that I found out that 'One Lug' wasn't musical, even in that one, and Stradivarius couldn't paint for toffee. I heard on the other hand about someone who bought a button for a pound and sold it for three thousand. Or was it that he bought three thousand buttons and sold the lot for a pound? Chinese whispers. 'Send three and fourpence. We're going to a dance.' (I'm going to explain that one because someone told me they couldn't find anyone who knew the 'golf tees' joke earlier in this book.) An infantry unit under heavy artillery fire in the trenches sent a runner with the message,

"Send reinforcements. We're going to advance."

By the time H.Q. got their message it had become,

"Send three and fourpence. We're going to a dance."

Chinese whispers abound in the car boot industry and, although bargains do exist, you may be lucky if you can buy something for a fiver that's actually worth four pounds fifty. It's not that the traders are being dishonest, but most of them haven't a clue what the true value is, so they take a wild guess and it's up to you to decide whether or not to buy. It's easy to know when a car boot sale is about to start because you can see the vultures circling. Oh no! That's when you know a lion has made a fresh kill when you are on safari. It's the same principle though. As the traders arrive you will regularly see the same faces every week peering through their car windows, looking for the magical bargain of the century. The bolder ones are rummaging in the boxes before the trader can even set up their tables. It's the occasional traders they're after - the ones who have genuinely cleared out their attic or their shed, and may have a little bit of treasure that they don't know the value of. A piece of Wade or Beswick may not look like much and might be sold on their stall for two or three pounds but it can fetch up to a hundred for the dealer at an antique sale. Who are the vultures? They're not regulars at Sotheby's - they are more often other car-booters who have gone to the trouble of reading up a bit on what is collectable. Perhaps I'm being unkind labelling them vultures. There's nothing immoral in what they are doing. The whole point of car boot sales is to look for bargains, and the more astute dealers have simply done their homework. It's not difficult to get in on the act. Go to your local library and read up on a few of the more popular collectables. Fine china, old fishing tackle, military items, books, records, ornaments, musical instruments. The list is endless and no-one is an expert on everything, but you can easily learn enough to be able to make yourself a bit of pin money.

The car-booters fall into very distinct categories, and it's as well to know which type you are buying from. The ones, who are there every week, may charge a bit more for the better items, but the advantage of buying from them is that, if you buy something which is faulty, they will usually refund in full if you take something back the following week. They are keen to keep you as a future customer. If they are using the market as a way of making at least part of their living, they are often quite enthusiastic about buying from you, if you have items which they can use for stock.   So, if you are having a clear out, and don't fancy the thought of standing at your own stall for the day, approach one of the regulars, and make them an offer they can't refuse. There's a second group of regulars who never buy stock, but simply try to recycle anything they can find in a skip or a bucket. I'll never really understand how they manage to raise enough money to pay for their stall, far less make a wage for the day, but they are there regularly, so I suppose it must be possible.

By far the most popular are the occasional stall holders, who not only have some really interesting, and even valuable stock, but also have no idea what they should charge for each item. Most of their worthwhile items will be sold in the first half-hour, so you will have to be there as soon as they arrive on the market, if you want to get in on the act.

Try a car boot sale yourself at some time. If you pick a day when the weather is good, it can be a rewarding and enjoyable experience, and it will give you an insight into how the whole system operates. Like most people you will probably start gathering your stock by rummaging through your cupboards and your shed but, before long, you will have to think where you can get some more stock .

There are lots of options available. Try some of the local auction sales. Invariably, there are job lots, which can be sifted through to top up your stall. It's worth spending a fair bit of time to sort out the better items, and to do a bit of cleaning and repairing, before you put them on your stall. The most difficult part for most people is the pricing, and strangely enough it can be made very simple if you have a few mail order catalogues to hand. Most of the goods you sell will be every day items whose second hand value is about half the new value. If you come across things which you feel may have a collector's value, don't be in too much of a hurry to put them on your stall. Make an occasional trip to a reputable auctioneer and you should find that valuations are free. If you have stumbled across a really valuable piece it is worth while putting it to auction, rather than trying to find a collector who will pay the price at your local car boot.

Not everyone who goes to car boot sales is a bargain hunter. Trading standards officers, police and social security fraud investigators could all find rich pickings and they all make occasional swoops. If I were selling regularly at a car boot sale, I would declare the extra income to the Inland Revenue. In fact, I would probably even exaggerate the income, so that I could pay a bit more tax than is really necessary. I've always wondered why any man would want to pay a P.V.C. clad woman to whip him, so perhaps paying the extra tax would give me some insight.

Chapter 11

Thinking Time

This chapter doesn't really exist, because I don't feel inclined to write anything at the moment. You may feel a bit peeved that you have paid for Chapter 11, but if it makes you feel any better, there's an important message in this non-existent section. It's quite possible to be so busy, that you fail to see that you're going in the wrong direction. Here are a few alternatives to consider:

1. Take ten minutes of 'THINKING TIME' every day to look at the big picture - I use an enlarged photograph of myself - it's very soothing.

2. Make one day of the week a 'non-working' day. It's important that your spouse doesn't consider this time available for household chores - it's 'THINKING TIME'. If you have problems in this area, it may be worthwhile investigating the brainwashing techniques used by political parties just before an election. Advanced students may be able to extend this procedure to six days a week.

3. Arrange a holiday for yourself in an exotic location. The Inland Revenue will be sympathetic to your claim that this is an important part of the strategic planning for your business, and will be happy to give full tax relief on your expenses. In the unlikely event that you should find a problem in this direction, you can keep your expenses to a minimum, by offering your services as a courier to airlines. They often need packages delivered by hand to various parts of the world.

"Can you take this vial of ram's semen to a sheep farm in the Northern Territory of Australia?"

"I'm sorry. I'm rather busy at the moment - Try Skippy the Kangaroo!"

On the other hand, if they want large suitcases of banknotes delivered to the Seychelles, make sure that the contract states, that you can keep the lot, if you have any difficulty finding the delivery address.

It is often possible to earn a little bit of extra money on the return flight, by bringing back Chippolata sausages. There are some businessmen in the Far East who will ask you to swallow the sausages whole, and pass them through your rectum, on your return to the U.K. Strangely, this method of transport seems to keep the sausages in excellent condition for the home market. The alternative method of transportation is 'mules', but airlines are reluctant to allow these animals to use passenger's seats. I would not recommend this sideline, as the sausages may have a high salt content, and if one should burst in your stomach, you could suffer severe heartburn.

4. Count all the money in your pockets. If this doesn't take very long, you definitely need more 'THINKING TIME.'

5. Think about all the money in other people's pockets, and work out a transfer strategy. Remember you have something they want.

6. Take a really hard look at yourself. Are you presenting the right image? Do people trust you? Do you dress for comfort, or do you try to make the statement - 'I'm right for this job.' Think about it. Are you a Scottish Tour guide in a kilt or a swimming instructor in a bowler hat?

Time to move on and do something. If you over-extend your 'THINKING TIME', you are no longer a thinker - you're a dreamer!

Chapter 12

Jump in quick - everyone is going to get rich

There always seems to be a get rich scheme in vogue at any particular time. Do you remember the Meat Parcels? Some enterprising butchers made up parcels of meat comprising a roasting joint or a chicken, a pack of bacon, sausages and various other bits and pieces. Every Tom, Dick or Harry, who had a car, then went door knocking and sold the parcels to housewives. When you got a chicken with one leg, you would be told that they were free-range chickens and your one must have caught its leg on a wire fence. When you got a pound of stuffing with a piece of steak you were well advised not to ask what you should do with it. Nothing wrong with all that so far. Through bulk selling, the butcher was able to keep the price down, and there was enough room for the door to door salesman to make a good wage, and still give a bargain pack to the housewife. The problem soon arose that the unsold parcels were taken home and frozen, then trotted out the next day to make their appearance again. Obviously the cars were not refrigerated and the parcels would eventually need a notice saying,

'Bargain pack of Salmonella'.

Much later on came the 'Convert your works pension' scheme. Suitable applicants (just about anyone who was breathing) were given a full twenty minutes training and sent out to con their friends into converting their pensions. Unfortunately, even the salesmen weren't aware of the eventual consequences for the customers, and it was a long time before the financial institutions behind the scheme received a rap on the fingers from the government, and were ordered to pay back the money that pensioners had lost. It came too late for some pensioners who died in the meantime.

Pyramid selling is another good example. You get ten of your friends to join and they each get ten of their friends to join and they each get ten of their friends to join and they each get ten of their friends to join... If you can get the Chinese government to discourage birth control this type of scheme has great possibilities.

The current vogue seems to be the World Wide Web. Recently I had someone say to me, "Everyone is making fortunes on the Web."

Not true. The fact is that some people are making fortunes on the Web, but then some people are making fortunes off the Web. If your product or idea is crap, it will be received with equal disdain locally or world-wide. I'm not knocking the idea of selling world-wide, but you must have something worthwhile to offer. Specialize! Not many of us are good at everything, (I'm not going to tell you the names of the others who are), so you have to offer something that your customer cannot get locally if you are going to succeed in this way. My own web-site www.scottishbordersbooks.co.uk is a typical example of specialization. The name of the site tells most of the story. On site you will see that Scottish Border books feature very strongly because many of the local authors visit my shop regularly, and I can therefore stock books which are less likely to get a mention nationally. A typical example, recently, was a book written by an eighty-year old retired farmer who wrote the story of his working life in the Borders. He spoke with an in-depth knowledge of the farms and the people over a period of his lifetime, and the story appealed to many people who knew him and recognised the land he loved. In fact the book was called 'The Land I Love'. He had the book printed locally, and only five hundred copies were produced. Most of them were sold in my shop within two months. A book like that might have appealed to homesick Borderers all over the world but, unfortunately, my web-site was not up and running at that time. It's never too late...I may feature it at some time on my site and, if there is enough response, I may be able to persuade him to go for a reprint.

The reason I feel that my particular web site can succeed is that Scots are great travellers. There has always been a strong tradition of doctors, engineers and soldiers who have sought their fame and fortune in foreign climes. The 'Bonnie Fighters' of Scotland have sold their services as mercenaries in battles throughout the world, and were greatly prized by their employers for their fighting skills and tenacity. At the end of many of these campaigns, the soldiers of fortune often settled in foreign lands, and, generations later, their descendants are keen to explore their distant heritage. It's hardly surprising that the Scots have a reputation as fighting men. From the earliest times, the inhabitants of this cold and often bleak country fought invaders and each other to survive. From the early days of the broadsword and the dirk to the sophisticated weaponry of modern warfare, Scotsmen have struck terror into the hearts of their enemies. It is worth noting that a disproportionately high number of men serving in the Special Forces of the British army are Scottish.

You can see my line of thinking. Now, what have you got to offer that has a potential audience world-wide? Get your thinking cap on again. It should never have been off in the first place. You should wear it even when you are in bed. Many of your best ideas will come to you before you nod off, and if you are over forty, some of them might even be money making ideas. Perhaps you will have inspiration when you are soaking in a hot bath or a Jacuzzi. Let your mind wander for a while, until you get the germ of an idea, then explore it further. If you don't come up with anything good, at least you will be the cleanest pauper in town.

Chapter 13
Spend, spend, spend.

I love starting a new chapter in this book. It's quite exciting ... I've no idea what's going to be in it, but I know that inspiration will arrive without warning. So much for forward planning, notes, etc. You've read twelve chapters now. Has your thinking changed at all? I hope that you are looking for opportunities and openings that haven't occurred to you before.

I was in my shop yesterday (Sunday) putting up some new shelves. The shop is usually open from Monday to Saturday only, but I left the front doors open while I was working. Kelso is quiet on a Sunday at this time of the year, but the little bit of trade that came my way while I was working, made me feel that I was getting my shelves for nothing. A visitor to the town popped in and asked me if I sold the 'Motor Trader'.

"I'm afraid not," I said, "but I have a very good second hand car for sale if you are interested."

It was worth a shot, but unfortunately he was looking for something in the ten thousand-pound range, and the car I was selling was about two thousand. I offered to charge him more but he declined. Ah well, you can't win them all, but, on the other hand, you can't win any of them if you don't try. The car in question is parked behind my house, and I don't use it, but it's not eating anything, and, at some time in the near future it may form part of a deal. Perhaps someone will offer me thousands of sets of darts or a dozen boa constrictors.

If you have already taken steps to making loads of money, maybe it's time to think about how you're going to hang on to it. I don't want to give the impression that a life of thrift is one that I would advocate. I really believe in enjoying life to the full and if that involves spending a bit, then, so be it. Sitting at home, counting it, loses its appeal very quickly, so, if you have pulled off a deal, then lash out and treat yourself. I like wine, women and song. My wife still lets me sing, anytime I want, which is very generous, because I'm a rotten singer. The main thing is not to spend all your hard-earned cash on your indulgences. Some of it should always be re-invested or laid aside to finance the next golden opportunity. It's a simple enough equation … spend a bit less than you earn, or, alternatively, earn a bit more than you spend. Do these two alternatives sound exactly the same? Not quite! How often have you heard people saying that they need every penny they earn, to buy the groceries and pay the bills? I agree they can't spend less than they earn, but the other alternative is always open to them. That's what this book is all about. It's common knowledge that we only use about ten per cent of our brain, so try using ten and a half per cent. (I don't want to put any strain on you by asking you to use your full potential.)

"I haven't got any spare time to earn any more."

You don't necessarily need more time, just a bit more thought. I've posed the question already. What have you got to offer ... Time? Talent? Capital? Energy? Beauty? Strength? A winning smile? A sympathetic ear? A big fat hairy ear? Everyone has got something. All you have to do is think how you can use it to your advantage. Incidentally, I've got no idea how you can make money by having a big fat hairy ear, but I'm not using a hundred per cent of my brain either, so perhaps I'm missing an opportunity, or even two.

It really hurt me typing that last sentence, so I took some time out and used another half per cent of my brain to dredge up a story about someone who profited from having a big fat hairy ear.

Many years ago there were two brothers who, sadly, were very challenged in the looks department. One brother had one big eye in the middle of his forehead and the other had a huge fat hairy ear. They were finding it very difficult to get work...hardly surprising as they kept applying for jobs as models on the catwalk. This was especially true of brother number two, who always wanted to model hats. Even the most creative millinery paled into insignificance when all eyes were on his big fat hairy ear. In desperation, they decided to run away to sea, and to this end they approached the captain of a British man-o-war and begged to be taken on to the crew. The captain was a bit reluctant at first, but agreed to take the first brother, Fred A. Stare, when he told him that he had always been the top pupil at his school. After a great deal of pleading, he relented and took on the second brother, Luggy Jim, as well. A few days into the voyage and the captain had a sudden flash of inspiration.

"Get up to the crows nest and look out for enemy ships," he said to Fred.

"Can I take my brother up there with me for company?" asked Fred.

"You might as well. He's good for nothing down here."

Early next morning there were excited screams from the crow's nest.

"Ship ahoy on the starboard bow," shouted Fred.

The captain rushed to the side of the ship (not easy for a man who was engrossed in trying to take a splinter out of his bum. There's not much to do at sea and the sailors invented their own games to pass the time. The previous night the captain had been drawn against the first mate Long John Silver in an arse-kicking competition), but he could see nothing. He pulled out a massive telescope and after much scanning he eventually noticed a tiny dot on the horizon.

"Are you sure it's a ship?" said he.

"Definitely! It's a French man-o-war," said Fred A. Stare

"You can't tell me that you can see the flags at that distance, even with your big eye."

"Of course not! Don't be silly! But my brother, Luggy Jim, can hear them speaking in French."

An observant customer, reading the script of my book in the shop, mentioned that he had noticed two references to casinos. (I could scarcely believe that anyone was paying that much attention ... I should have asked him to check my spelling and punctuation while he was at it.)

"Why would anyone who doesn't believe in wasting money be in a casino in the first place?" It's not as daft as it may seem. Casinos (not all of them) can be the most glamorous places in the world. The glistening white piano bar in the casino in the square in Monte Carlo, or the plush blue and gold surroundings of the former palace at St. Julian's in Malta, are sights you would never forget. Even in Britain, where the gaming board forbids stage entertainment, or drinks inside the gaming room, many of the better casinos make tremendous efforts to make the place comfortable and welcoming. Life membership is usually free of charge, the food in the restaurant is excellent and usually costs a lot less than the equivalent meal elsewhere, and, quite often, the casino has free buffet nights for members and guests. The Castle casino in Blackpool, although not one of the biggest, is the friendliest club I have ever been in. I visit the place only two or three times a year, and yet I am greeted like a long lost friend every time I appear there. They even send their members birthday cards and Christmas cards. They have dates of birth from the membership applications, and I suspect they have figured out for themselves when Christmas is. The casinos lay on all these treats because they are owned and run by philanthropists who want everyone to be happy. You don't believe me? You're right. The object of the exercise is to encourage you to gamble and lose your money. Losing isn't compulsory, but in the long run there are very few winners. The logic is simple...the odds in every game are stacked slightly in the house's favour. On the roulette wheel there are thirty-seven numbers (including zero) and the casino pays out thirty five to one (that's thirty-six chips including your stake) to the winners on a single number bet, so the odds are about 2.7% in the house's favour. There are lots of different bets you can make covering sections of the wheel, but the odds of winning remain pretty much the same. That's not a massive advantage for the house on a single bet, but if you sit at the table and bet repeatedly, it's enough to ensure that the staff get paid, and the shareholders in the casino will be paid dividends. The odds in another popular casino game, Blackjack, vary between one and seven per cent in the house's favour, depending on how well or badly you play. So, am I saying that's it's impossible to win? Of course not! Many players will have winning nights, but few, (very, very few) will win in the long run. What really amazes me is how badly many people play. It's not all that difficult to learn enough to be able to limit your losses, or even break even in the long run, and any small losses you do incur can be considered as part of the expense of an enjoyable night out. I certainly don't intend to teach you how to be a winner, (not in this book anyway.) The casino has made every effort to lay on the facilities for you to have a good night out, so don't spoil it by losing more than you can afford.

Chapter 14
A sight to behold

Do you always carry a camera? Let me re-phrase the question. Have you ever seen anything interesting? Many of the most famous photographs in the world, and believe me they are worth a great deal of money, were not taken by professionals, but were caught by someone who just happened to be passing at the time. This is equally true of video footage and stills.

Professional photographers are always on the lookout for leads, so that they can be on the spot when celebrities are likely to make an appearance, but no-one can anticipate the unusual situations that can be captured on film by the lucky amateur.

So why is a photograph so important compared with a good narrative description? No doubt you've heard the phrase 'A picture paints a thousand words.' I almost burst into song when I typed that phrase, but I resisted in case an audio version of this book is released. I was right at the front of the line when big noses were being handed out, but I was pushed aside by Barbara Streisand and Barry Manilow when the voices were distributed. It's an interesting experiment to try. Take a photograph or a short piece of video film and ask a few of your friends to write a thousand words describing the scene, after a very brief look. A great deal will be missed altogether, like expression on faces, colours, clothing etc. and you will find huge differences in the details that different eye-witnesses observe. Picasso may have noticed the lady with three breasts and an ear growing out of her arm, but the next observer could have missed that if he was a bit of a leg man. A passing American policeman may have said,

"I saw some lads having a bit of good natured rough and tumble, and Rodney King was enthusiastically joining in."

The expression 'Seven colours of s—t' may not have appeared in his report, but, study the video footage and I doubt if you will see Rodney King's face appearing from the mêlée wearing a big grin.

The Rodney king footage was shown on television screens throughout the world, and stills taken from the video were front page in every newspaper. The person responsible for making the film would receive payment each time it was used. Did the film-maker follow Rodney King around waiting for it to happen? No! He just happened to be there, but, more importantly, he happened to have a camera with him.

Another classic piece of video film, which recently made a big splash on the news programmes, showed a silverback gorilla comforting a little boy who had fallen into the enclosure. What a human-interest story that was - and it was filmed by a tourist who just happened to be there, and again, who *happened to have a video camera*.

Wow! A daffodil in February. That's unusual.

There are two ways you can go about making money from sensational photographs. Firstly, you can try to be in the right place e.g. If you want to get the earth shattering shot of the Loch Ness monster, there's no point in hanging around Trafalgar Square, unless you have an exceptional tele-photo lens. Spending a bit of time at the side of Loch Ness might prove worthwhile, and, in fact, one chap has lived in a caravan at the side of the loch for several years waiting for Nessie to make him rich and famous. So far, this ploy has only made him cold and damp. The alternative I suggest is to carry a camera with you at all time, and capture any event, which would interest the newspapers. It may not be of national or international importance, but your shot could still earn you a fair bit, if you sell it to a publication with specialist or local interest themes. Last year, I stopped the car to watch a rabbit chasing a stoat and giving it a right towsing. The action went on for fully three minutes, and I sat there really enthralled. I've studied wildlife since I was a lad, and this was quite the most fascinating sight I had ever seen. I'm ashamed to say I didn't have a camera with me, but if I had been able to capture that sequence, I know I could have sold it to any country magazine or nature programme.

Generally speaking, the amateur photographs, which are likely to sell, are shots of momentary events, which are sensational, like disasters, crashes and fires. Scenes which remain unchanged, are the domain of the professional photographer, who can choose the lighting and the angles to get better photographs.

I spoke to a lady recently, who had taken my advice seriously and was carrying her camera, when she was fortunate enough to meet a group of aliens from outer space. They had very obligingly posed for photographs, and it was just unfortunate that she forgot to take off the lens cover when she was shooting. The resulting photographs were not one hundred per cent clear, but she was able to give a very good description of the event in about one thousand words.

Chapter 15
How do you think I got my 97 pence?

When I thought about this chapter it was so full of good ideas that I decided to keep them all to myself. I may have taught you everything you know, but you can't expect me to teach you everything that I know.

Have fun - Be happy - Make money.

DO NOT REMOVE THIS TOKEN FROM THE BOOK

TAKE THIS BOOK ALONG WITH YOU TO THE TOURS - THIS PAGE MUST BE REMOVED BY THE TOUR STAFF

Auld Reekie Tours
45 Niddrie Street
Edinburgh
Tel: 0131 557 4700
Web site www.auldreekietours.co.uk
E-mail auldreekietours@blueyonder.co.uk

THIS VOUCHER ENTITLES 2 PEOPLE FREE ENTRY TO THE WITCHCRAFT, UNDERGROUND AND GHOST TOURS.

Please telephone or e-mail to book in advance.